C000016217

Carlisle in Haiku Form

First Impressions

David Simmons

Carlisle in Haiku Form: First Impressions by David Simmons
First Edition

ISBN: 978 1 9163881 3 0

First published in the UK in 2021 by Caldew Press.

Caldew Press
Tolivar
12 St George's Crescent
Carlisle
CA3 9NL

caldew-press@outlook.com
www.caldewpress.com

CALDEW PRESS

Foreword

Men and women in Japan have been writing haiku for well-nigh 400 years. Millions are written world-wide and some poets write thousands. Young kids today write excellent haiku poems in school. Writing them in English, it's a way of knowing how words are formed of syllables, the sound of vowels alongside consonants.

I listened to local poet John Chambers read from his book, *Haiku: Poems Beyond the Mountain*, inspired by the Lake District. A brief chat followed. He gently warned me that writing haiku can be addictive. I decided to have a go myself, with the knowledge that a few well-chosen words can be very powerful.

During the process of composing a poem, I often say the words out loud to myself. It's like a rehearsal. The rhythm and sound are important. I think my best poems give voice to the subject matter. They demand a life off the page, to be performed. Some singing may be required.

My poem, 'Chanting in the name of Lorna Graves', provides an example of giving that voice. It did well at the local Borderlines Poetry

Competition in 2018. That recognition heartened me. I felt in some way indebted to Carlisle, the city I had lived and worked in for 40 years.

Alongside writing, I enjoy composing photographic images that speak to me. Although I haven't studied art, I think there's always been an artistic side seeking an outlet. I came to writing haiku late but very quickly started to write them onto fabric strips, thereby creating visual accessibility. At the time, I was writing a lengthy poem about the city. When I changed to writing the poem in haiku form, I realised the poems provided snapshots of the city.

To capture the bigger picture I would have to write hundreds of haiku, and that's what I did. Handwritten onto white cotton tape, with a distinctive red dot, the poems had an immediate visual impact, and the project *Carlisle in Haiku form* was born.

I learnt that in Japan haiku were traditionally written vertically. I chose to display my cotton tapes informed by the Japanese traditions of *tokonoma*, *kintsugi* and *furoshiki*. The white cotton tapes became the source of several local art installations and exhibitions in 2019. They filled a gazebo at the Carlisle Unity Festival and draped the pagoda in Bitts Park. They contributed to *The Gate* exhibition and formed a solo exhibition along the south aisle of Carlisle Cathedral.

The widening content of haiku has evolved over time. Modern haiku are a very adaptable, flexible form of poetry. Some even omit the traditional *kigo*, the seasonal reference.

Haiku tend to hold a certain honesty or poetic truth. I hope mine do too. These poems present a poetic view of Carlisle. Haiku also tend to capture a moment in time, a thought or an idea. Perhaps the haiku you are about to read will give you cause to pause and consider.

In selecting my haiku for this book, I wanted to provide a narrative, a story that mirrors the city, making a connection from one haiku to the next. I have tried to give a first impression for someone new to the city. And for those familiar with the city, perhaps a fresher, wider perspective.

There is a purpose too in the illustrations. They may contain the gaze of many lifetimes, scenes we pass every day without a second thought. Perhaps there is something not noticed before.

Composing the poems entailed much walking. Many bus rides too. It's been good for my body and soul. My affection for Carlisle has deepened.

As you read the poems I hope a little of that affection lingers, rests on you, and encourages you to become better acquainted with this city on the doorstep of the Lake District, this wonderful Border City.

Carlisle in Haiku
poems that transcend the page
fear not and be just

After you have read the poems, or someone has kindly read the book to you, I've left a small space below the last haiku as an invitation to continue the story. Perhaps you'd like to fill it with a drawing or haiku. If this is not your own book, seek permission, or start on a scrap of paper; have a go.

Contents

Footsteps to the past

in the beginning
from the garden of Eden
a city was born

flow north south east west
willows shade the sandy banks
Romans bathe their sores

Ricard the rider
post ala petriana
Norman Knight farmer

oak tree-rope dangles
swings high above the Eden
peaceful cattle graze

Augustine Hippo
attendant angels guide you
to this Holy throne

reiver families
carved in stone by Bishop's curse
harsh names realign

Citadel stronghold
lowly pawns guard Kings and Queens
safer to castle

Jacobite inmates
licked all traces of dampness
from solid stone walls

sweep of coping stones
hands brush soft tight warm moss fleece
in praise of west wall

flat-capped Rudd women
trade on steps of market cross
Caldew bed red stone

smiths tanners skinners
shoemakers tailors weavers
old Guildhall ghost hunt

canal navvies drink
plundering the Fox and Grapes
coal becomes cheaper

five poor skeps of meal
on feast of Saint Nicholas
leper hospice treat

in Union workhouse
Lodge Chapel Infirmary
from birth to Uni

canal terminus
horse drawn Basin turns to rail
watering station

the hanky steam shed
depot of Upperby men
working the railway

milling families
the city of the waters
drapers and dealers

Dixon built his streets
workers plied the Milbourne Arms
and the Woolpack Inn

old Rickergate blues
Bobbies protected and served
pints at Malt Shovel

from handloom weavers
to whirr of the bobbin wheel
shuttle buzz and click

Electric lighting
accompanies Metal Box
hum thrum to bog road

cotton spin dye print
when fifteen factories flowed
Caldew powered mill

Byron Shakespeare Burns
street poets of the city
crowded Caldewgate

Chaplain of great war
Theodore Bayley Hardy
bookshop pen and sword

a first for Carlisle
female Oxford graduate
our Norah Hartley

seeping November
poppies silent affection
red red remember

In praise of buildings

blood red silhouettes
hard against warm sandstone walls
weeping poppies fall

embrace heritage
display our repairs with pride
Kintsugi Carlisle

stepways to heaven
first port of call old Town Hall
lovingly restored

seven bay façade
dated lead rainwater heads
best downspouts in town

this place where we live
the art we create and the
objects we cherish

sandstone is redressed
around the Southwell style door
this fabric wears well

big Fratry invite
to the less able alike
new access welcome

close with Saint Cuthbert
forever on a journey
with prayers to God

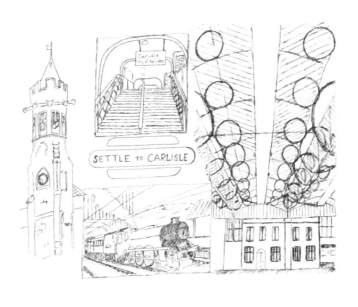

light stone Citadel
of Olympic proportions
go and meet your dreams

red orange maroon
Dixon's chimney smokes once more
winter sunset wisps

shaddon mill rejig
sandstone dress on bare girders
seeks industry chic

referendum blue
Border Kirk is scots for church
hire tartan next door

pithy message boards
an oasis of Elim
pointers from Saint Paul

bold as Saint Aidan
tubas reverberate brass
solemn rafters sound

gothic with Saint John
orchestra's strings stretch out to
underfloor heating

in C sharp minor
Leah plays Saint Barnabas
tames the Humoreske

Saint James' lacrosse team
Keen three year olds tears of joy
milk their victory

immaterial
when shoes are taken off
an Imam welcomes

Central Plaza crime
honest Crown took all rooms then
left without paying

matinee high tea
stay for old Post office pint
Halston's Penny Blue

Working their socks off

men tek hod and sway
Cumberland Westmorland style
done wearing long johns

farm work sleep repeat
foot and mouth never repeat
farm work sleep repeat

second hand Thursday
implements criss cross the floor
two bid two bid four

Linton pattern piece
to Takisada Japan
wool cotton number

the K is for knit
the ang is for angora
the ol is for wool

Kangol became Breed
long seatbelt testing machine
students now have keys

interdependent
multidisciplinary
University

down Lowthians lane
refuge of a fair trade world
no place for racism

working with awaz
spell diversification
multicultural

make for Millers meals
rooted like vegetables
in the market hall

our cracker packers
cannot hear themselves talking
women say me too

yellow custard creams
hundreds thousands bucketloads
count broken biscuits

little steps big step
nursery whets appetite
school in September

prism means potential
all abilities create
art gives therapy

in Glenmore we trust
happiness comes through Heathlands
empowering us

green back lane artist
blends in garage door mural
stanwix banksy lass

budding carpenters
no dead wood in Dentonwood
carving out a life

for risking their lives
claps cloak windows doorways roads
our world saviours

homely Hospice nurse
always wants the best for you
our lifelines eased through

downhill from the church
cheers to The old Brewery
in The Joiners Arms

talk of Pirelli
recruiting operatives
in The Cranemakers

whinnying engines
in old biscuit works stables
Saab car horsepower

Angela Vera
turns left off English street, yo!
my favourite truck

B and M Bargains
is Woolworths store more or less
miss pick n mix sweets

screw and fix your home
tap businesses in Kingstown
with perfect pencils

elderly lady
Kindly distributed sweets
happy bus drivers

Play can be magic

bus sixty seven
family to Hammond's pond
ducks ask for picnic

smiling nan with pram
many thanks said to driver
busy bus chatter

hear xylophones play
up pop tulips and ice cream
free fireworks display

see pantomime sign
civic Beauty and the Beast
our Hardwicke circus

naughty cricketer
sat bottom step of clubhouse
threw wicket away

Dan can Karate
can do razzamataz too
play can be magic

with integrity
persevere for self control
fit in Taekwondo

gan ower field mam
promise not to climb the slide
be back for teatime

extravaganza
youth zone hosts bazaar weekend
multicultural

Radio weekend
we dance and sing along to
ga ga ooh la la

high tide time shortly
traffic news weather sport then
play three little dings

damn cold and losing
sat at floodlit Brunton Park
eat warm pie with dad

recall of The Pools
all our clothes nicked from lockers
left with bare basics

Kids eat drink chatter
computers find the answer
bored books watch from shelves

four saxophonists
busk under the Christmas lights
in school uniform

ping pong ping pong ping
point set match win glad lose sad
dark locked cold church hall

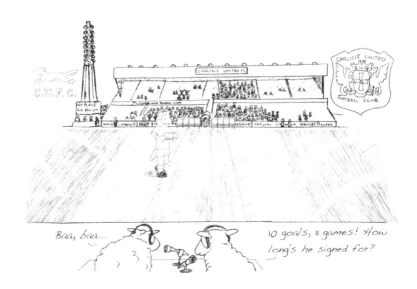

Baa, baa...

10 goals, 11 games! How long's he signed for?

Keenan park Zen art
goalposts crossbar a flutter
flags pray for football

This is Brunton Park
touch going down the tunnel
be just and fear not

cold wet paddock blues
backsides stand against the wind
sheep quietly bleat

sheep have gone sheepish
less unseen two rivers meet
track the fleet of feet

all weather terrain
slick moonlit line of wheelers
runners colour town

walk with Hadrian
stroll chin up through daffodils
to and fro Bowness

seek Edward the First
secret salmon Haafnetters
take the Solway tour

viewed from the backside
this lifelike Border Reiver
is less forbidding

Laal touch of mousse spray
Limousin cross hairdresser
wins and pins rosette

racecourse bell and belles
dress first and place a flutter
hot tips for best hat

miss the smell of youth
searching for the sex pistols
the feel of vinyl

on the piano
leah and Alicja
follow Noriko

actress designs set
bloody marvellous murder
suspects in green room

red tower nightwatch
bailed out of bed slipped down pole
leaving bar and art

follow charcoal line
to Maryport and Parton
with Percy Kelly

read Cumbrian books
browse cakes and garden poems
sup Management ale

prose and poetry
season of over-ripe fruit
Borderlines is here

world at fingertips
sublime poetry and wine
mellows group gossip

I think in haiku
therefore I am a haiku
Basho to Descartes

mindful Kintsugi
happily embrace your faults
become beautiful

Haiku for Carlisle
poems embrace the city
two cultures collude

mindful Kintsugi
happily embrace your faults
become beautiful

centre your Karma
meditate the day away
Uma Kadampa

Ahmed fries his fish
served with homemade tartare sauce
salom alaikum

Aris says gyros
now try sokalatina
briki greek coffee

Russian caravan
Watt's coffee house trip to taste
worldwide loose leaf tea

slope to haggis scones
see you start New Year in Whytes
to celebrate Burns

summer fruit crumble
Mary has famous puddings
seniors lick their lips

walk down Denton Holme
call bingo shout house for joy
perms cloud full bus home

suspended coffees
kindness not a miracle
in the Cornerhouse

in the port road straits
there's a jovial sailor
what shall we do with ....

beware friday night
Botchardgate barrier closed
pastors befriend drunks

that William Rufus
third son of the Conqueror
restores our city

letters in English
from friends in Flensburg and Slupsk
Europe keeps in touch

It's in our nature

painted by Turner
conceived by Sir Robert Smirke
humble Eden bridge

Eden sentinel
silent silver quickening
Heron catches fish

full bony glory
our dinosaurs roamed on land
but Driggsby was beached

elder fisherman
now claims he wooed a grayling
Lady of the stream

blink of Kingfisher
on Waverley viaduct
will not miss a train

rude hare pees on tracks
in disused marshalling yard
ears V sign to trains

taking your chances
hopeful crocus hug the ground
braving the west wind

daffodils parade
Easter bells renew faith days
peals wander as clouds

pink blossom spreads joy
onto passing retinas
blink and you miss it

bright lonely tube cloud
we claim our new volutus
Helm bar wind be damned

south east Keenan wind
north wind Bitts west wind Morton
east wind Melbourne park

swan duck two ducks ducks
birds sing sun shimmers water
train next stop café

give nature a go
play in the woods at Watchtree
mind the bicycles

wife of Emperor
bathing leg before wicket
Romans bowled over

cats and dogs cool paws
kids swelter to the river
temper   gauges toil

sometimes you can hear
the sweet crack of bat on ball
above the birdsong

this year's green space team
best urban community
blooming marvellous

twenty minute train
tarn walk from Brampton junction
Talkin of beauty

bus ticket explores
Silloth's long green seafront lawn
lone fishing boat trawls

Glenridding by bus
I had Place Fell to myself
High Street was empty

shed brew breaks sun's strength
amongst allotment showers
vegetables bear fruit

Watt of Knowefield wood
nurseryman to the Manx
farm seeds to the Queen

problem with sneezeweed
tending Morton manor lawns
use handkerchief tree

bark becomes a face
when dusk engraves the churchyard
devil of a shock

burnished acorns graze
husks haunt Uni grounds in fall
best art and design

angelic delight
find beyond the darkest door
Hail winter hazel

FOR RISKING THEIR LIVES

yuletide rainbow glows
arching Saint John's tall tower
lean gravestones applaud

rivers borrow plains
rain rain unglorious rain
never repeat that

criss cross the Caldew
find Hydrometry levels
askew on Skew bridge

flood alert on red
Environment agency
trusts its barriers

nothing is ignored
the water wolf bullies doors
and slips under floors

households kettled high
they wade through waterlogged minds
as the dank dirt cloaks

off Debenhams shore
an alligator patrols
seeking Babyland

will never grow old
cute tree baby held in arms
awaits higher flood

Advent door now sealed
that number five storm Desmond
not an act of God

lone mulberry tree
missing old friend tulip tree
now fancies Fratry

schoolgate protesters
children demand guardians
walk to hybrid bus

thoughts pollute the skies
every time you fly with
aviation oil

Kiss Kiss nose to tail
cars go bumper to bumper
faster walkers wave

Eycott Hill by bike
and we are like babies in
sphagnum moss nappies

solar wind wave tide
Solway city greenest dream
citizens buy it

try Furoshiki
wrap in wool or cotton cloth
go eco friendly

wearing the city
on our bodies on our sleeves
in the air we breathe

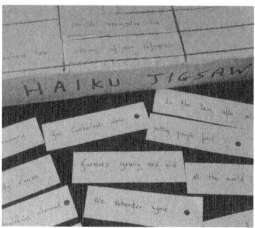

Unity Festival, Carlisle City Centre, 13th July 2019

Pagoda, Bitts Park, August 2019

Carlisle Cathedral, October 2019

Carlisle in Haiku form is on Facebook

https://www.facebook.com/Carlisle-Haiku-581393239045854/

Carlisle in Haiku form at Unity Festival 2019
can be watched on Vimeo at:

https://vimeo.com/354540716

Acknowledgements

Many people have helped me bring the whole project, *Carlisle in Haiku form*, to fruition. Here, I would like to thank the following people for their help specifically with creating this book.

Philip Hewitson and Susan Cartwright-Smith who, as Caldew Press, guided, supported and encouraged me throughout in its design and content.

The same Philip Hewitson for his drawings, bringing to life, and enhancing, my ideas for the illustrations.

Tony Hendry, fellow poet, for his observations and assistance in helping me select, from numerous haiku, those to include in the book.

Becca Roberts for her proofreading, valued warm comments and wise suggestions, all absorbed to provide better readability.

John Clare, early 19th century agricultural labourer and poet. A recent reading of *The Shepherd's Calendar* (Oxford University Press, 1964) confirmed my thoughts on including handwritten poems in their original form, just as they were written, with their characterful spelling, punctuation and grammar, as a social and historical record.

The Japanese tradition of *kintsugi*, originating from the repair of pottery, guiding me throughout the haiku project to display and embrace my faults.

Thank you to *SpeakEasy Magazine* for publishing, in Issue no 4, some of the haiku, particularly those having a church theme.

'Burnished acorns graze' and 'Will never grow old', were published in a similar version in *Mind Trees of the Urban Forest.*

Biography

David's favourite childhood memories are of summer holidays. Weeks spent at his grandmother's farm-house in the Eden Valley. His mother was raised there on what had been a small tenant farm.

Failing his eleven-plus exam while living on the south coast did him a favour. He played every sport going at his secondary school and was an avid reader, especially of Thomas Hardy: his life, Wessex novels and poetry. Inspired by Hardy, David took to letter writing in his teens as a means to share his thoughts and experiences, a practice he continues to this day. Passing A levels at grammar school, he went on to obtain a degree in psychology at what was then Newcastle upon Tyne Polytechnic. He moved to Carlisle to work and has lived in the city ever since.

When long-term physical problems curtailed outdoor activities and sporting life, he used writing to maintain mental wellbeing. In recovery, countering social isolation, he was welcomed by Gwenda and Lucy to Bookends poetry and book groups.

David was jolted into performing his poetry after seeing soldiers patrol the city streets following the floods in 2015.

His poem 'Chanting in the name of Lorna Graves', in remembrance of the Cumbrian artist, was runner-up in the 2018 Borderlines Poetry Competition.

CALDEW PRESS

caldew-press@outlook.com
www.caldewpress.com

Printed in Great Britain
by Amazon